# ONE LIFE SO MANY DREAMS

## LIVED AND EXPERIENCED

### BY

### LAYTON

ISBN: 1-4107-2965-6 (e-book)
ISBN: 1-4107-2966-4 (Paperback)

This book is printed on acid free paper.

E-Mail: Layton@for-layton.com
or visit me @ www.for-layton.com

1stBooks – rev. 07/01/03

# Prelogy

Webster says that a eulogy is all about "higher praise", it didn't mention anything about death or funeral days, but just like always we understand things as they are and never want for change, I'm not the same, so I want to lead my on so it can be real, I just want the world to know me, that's why I call this my Prelogy.

I wont tell you I am some fantastic guy that is all about love, I am but no one knows me or even bothers' to ask what I'm thinking of; I made a way for myself without being accepted by those that call me their friend; there were a few that didn't pretend. I never learn to trust so I never let friends in. I was forced to go to church and pray, forced to work as a child and never receive any pay oh my fault because they would say, I clothe you and feed you, shelter you everyday. But I was a child and I just wanted to play; learn from my big brother but he never had the time. Told me he never wanted that job, I was the reason that he left home I was a child just here alone. So I learned those street things; in that world you gotta be real. Still, so many fake asses hiding behind glass's or fake social worker credentials, which was my existence because those that I wanted to love me only showed me distance. Please believe me, please listen don't just skim the lines for rhythms please feel the feelings, this world is all about dealings real or not like it or not this world is all we got. Make your own heaven; hell like that flame is burning hot, my world didn't change until I stop being the same, understanding this game this is my Prelogy now do you remember my name.

Please believe this just feel this; the world as it has been brought to me, loveless is not the same as not having love from family, they did show love to me conditional as it was. Being a nephew or a cousin just hanging around, I found I wasn't missing anything I always had enough; there was always someone willing to whip my but. To them that was love that was suppose to enough, so I learn to learn everything I came into contact with was a lesson earned. If it was money I was in it, I did it, if it was straight I bent it to fit my needs, I was a preteen and introduced to drinking and weed everybody that I knew was that way so that's what I grew to need, what a teen believes. There's really no need to feel sad, and family please don't get mad, I learned to turn that drama into a winner; I been around for a while but I feel like a beginner, still a sinner I'm just real in my world and not a pretender. *One Life So Many Dreams* this is just me, this is my on **Prelogy.**

**Remember the Four L's Live-Love-Laugh and Layton**

**Peace**

# Fire and Ice

I'm on a mission, I need you to listen wanna tell you about my life, feel my story filled with fire and ice, filled with a brother wanting to do right. But want never follows the right track, missing any kind of direction, starving for knowledge wanting affection. Just wanting to keep my shit together, reality was talking never.

I'm walking I just feel I could do better I just want to roll and spread some cheddar. But here comes sex and sin complicating shit crossing my eyes making my knees bend. But then again that's what I wanted, no shame in my game I never fronted, thought I was macking, thought I was the shit I was what was happening. Only in my mind if you too sleepwalk you too will find life is a cycle and I was riding high. My life was passing me by. Quick through life means quick to die close you bag up zip goodbye. But this is my life so don't cry for me, just try like me to live and be happy. Jealous fools want let peace be, then there's chance and the wrong opportunity. My life's cycle is down more misery. Fuck that I don't need the company but that's the fire and ice in life and that's how life be.

02-25-02

# A Black Family

Today through pain I grow, not knowing just going, because I
    was told to do so
All confused, feeling misused, abused, I loose before I enter, and
    everyday is like winter
It seems as if I'm a beginner, a true sinner, so I turn, my turn,
    turns me to you, it's true
You're not just a dream you're real, I feel you near, it's clear to
    me, I see, you see
Life as it is, not as it is to me, so be you, and we'll be what we
    were meant to be,
As long as it's clear and you hear my heart calling it's stalling,
    true player falling
No longer ballling or tricking outside, no longer living just to lust
    and lie, I'll try
To be living and giving to you, a true man, who can, believe and
    lead a family
For you and me, that's what we be, a black family, a black family

A family I thought only existed, on TV or in some history, so I
    listen, now listen
We both know this show, is a onetime blessing, so I'm guessing,
    just checking.
This is more than a fun and sun summer, this is real to me, a thrill
    to me, no drama
Why you being so quiet, are you hiding, no I'm paranoid. I have
    wrecked the joy
I have ignored, the obvious before my eyes, you're with me and
    you're the prize
Why then you say have I jeopardized, but I have realized, your
    presence says,
You're satisfied, that smile just can't hide your warmth says what
    words can't deny
I riding high on this life and this love on my mind, it's great this
    fate to find

2

My queen that shapes my heart and soul, truth be told, I'm glad
    you grabbed a hold
To be giving and living with you, lucky me and my family, can
    you see this be
My history, my life, my legacy it started with you and me. And
    now we're a
**Black Family**

# Are You Down with Me?

I'm hearing you, you're calling but stalling, I'm feeling you, but
  what can I do
Can we exists, me and you, seems just as if, none of this is real to
  me
I have to ask if this is what it seems to be, or am I crazy
Or am I your love because I made things easy, from easy to
  pleasing
From pleasing to needing, that leaves me believing, or
I'm left wondering but hoping, barely coping, is this ending
You see, I'm finding, I'm needing, you here with me
But I have to know, are you down with me, down with me

Let me break this down, if you're down you're down
If I drown, you drown I'm you in every conceivable way
You gotta be me, blindly, and you can't stray
If my sun turns gray, I'm lost, and we have only grief
You have to know in me is relief, in me you have unending belief
When you hurt, out of sync or just don't feel like yourself
Can't get going life is showing you peace is with someone else
You may be tempted, you're human, but you gotta see
It ain't easy but it's pleasing, now are you down with me, down
  with me

I know that together, we can weather, anything but time
If you want life, like this, I'm offering you peace of mind
I wanna give you a world of diamonds, and warm sandy beaches
I wanna dine you, and wine you, show you love that Allah teaches
I wanna take all your troubles in my hand, let me stand you pain
Let me shield you from your rain, let me love you over and over
  again
I wanna show you tenderness, true this, true that, yes true love
I wanna be who you think of, I wanna be your definition of love
Now tell me is this how you want your life to be
Now I have to know, you have to show are you down with me,
  down with me?

# Are You the One??

I know you're careful, for love is special
You wanna be the queen and I wanna give you everything
I'll be your king, but there's this thing, a ring
No, a place in your heart, to be a part, can we start
Or do we need time, to find our own corner
To keep our family stronger, not for now but for longer
Eternality calls for our existence, but I feel resistance
You're just so pretty I could have missed this
Thinking with my eyes on the prize blinking
Dodging that ever present feeling of sinking
Yet forever we should be joined, a phrase coined
Our hearts linking, each of us as one never to be undone
And it's from, my heart that I am saying
That I'm not playing are you, am I the one
Never, ever to be neglected
Out of all the women in the world, it seems you're the one
If I'm the one that you have selected
A lifetime with you is what's expected
A lifetime with you and I'll never regret it
Leaving you oh no forget it
Am I, are you the one, are you the one?

# Believe

I think how can this be, she's with me, loving me
Like a dream a fantasy, pure ecstasy, you see
In our games the things, I chose to, I chose you
I'm not like anything that you're use to, I'm here for you
I want to elevate your mind until we find, entwined
That level of proof is truth that to many is unkind
I just want to show you things that to you are special
I'll be gentle but firm, sensuous, and oh so careful
That in your world, next to the girls, I'll be your reason
For living, for breathing, I want to make your life pleasing
Open your mind, and heart so you can see, see me
We can live this fantasy; it can be, can you believe

All that is good I'll bring to you, I'll do for you, if you
Keep doing the things that you do, that thing you do
That draws me to you, like glue, let's just live and laugh
Let's just enjoy what we have, this minute, this second
I'll never leave you long, never leave you guessing
If I do or don't if I will or wont, I'll be there I care
Never having anything but smiles to share, can we go there
To that level of mental bliss a kiss make a wish,
Anything you need just believe in me, just believe in this,
If you only believe in what you see take a look, believe in me
We can live this fantasy, you and me, can you believe

# Can You See the Light

Can You See The Light
(This click is tight it feels right)

This grief I thought to be was just a brief test for me, to see
If I am a man, or just a lesson to understand, I didn't let it get out
    of hand
My plan was based on my life, 6-trey lessons and racial strife
Not to mention two ex-wives, but I finally got it right, now
When you see me you see me I'm grinning, I'm spending, simply
    winning
Just trying to keep my world spinning this click feels like a brand
    new beginning

Can You See The Light
(This click is tight it feels right)

This isn't magic I didn't let the madness throw me off, I try not to
    think
About all the shit I lost, the cost of wanting to succeed, The hurt
    when you realize in a fool you believed, I was grown but I was
    still naïve, my bad but I have a way to get
What I need, I feel sad but in the real world there's no make
    believe, America was built by taking what was needed from
    the have-not's to the greedy, or is that seedy
Any way you stack it success can make you sleazy I watch my
    back trying to keep
My world pleasing

Can You See The Light
(This click is tight it feels right)

Ain't no reason for the heartache if you want to go let's just
    break, don't need
An explanation I was there I know the situation, but everybody's
    got a story

To tell, a lie to live, a stint in hell but I don't owe you shit for
    sleeping with me
Keeping me company that's just how shit be, you had no trouble
    spending my
Money enjoying the milk and honey, It's a sad day when lovers
    can't be friends
I don't mind you leaving but ain't no me and you again, you
    wanted out
So just know ain't no coming back in

**Can You See The Light**
**(This click is tight it feels right)**

# ...For Me

I wish there was a chance just to one time feel romance, or
To fly and feel the wind, I want to feel the warmth of sex without
    sin
I want to know that what I hear is true; I want to be able to trust
    you
I want to wish that you still loved me; I realize that that's my
    fantasy
So I open my eyes to the prize, I'm living this life why jeopardize
My time, my mind I don't need another—for me to find
My heaven, my peace with self, I ain't trying to hear from no one
    else

I just want from me, for me to feel free
Nothing complicated, no bull instigated
I just want from me, for me to be
I just want for me to feel free

I work my job; sob got me really working hard
Making money for him, sweating the drama and skim
A dime or two, love the cam, but I just don't give a damn
I am blessed just to be, so why you wanna try and stress me
I just can't figure out, but I can I know what this is about
Self destruct, or just walk out, or stay and sweat and pout
I'll tell you what I'm gonna do, what ever I feel up to
Whatever makes me smile and forget, about all this grit
And grim on my mine, it's time to have a good time

I just want from me, for me to feel free
Nothing complicated, no bull instigated
I just want from me, for me to be
I just want for me to feel free

# Forget About You

I want peace for me. This hurt to cease to for me
But you tease me, then pretend that it's pleasing, I see
My thoughts, my mind, my time, I was caught, I fought
I forgot everything that I was taught. My fault, here I go.
Into a world that I thought I knew. Being played, being used
So why choose, this path when I know I'll lose, that makes me a
     fool
Or am I cool, I lost because I broke the golden rule, playing the
     part
I need a woman that has my best interest at heart. A woman
That can jump start my heart. Since you can't this is where we
     part

Ain't no sunshine at times and you're here, sky's are clear
We just have different path, but mine brings me back here
I do love you, but it's true, every smile is not a laugh
We are two hearts but not equal halves. That's sad.
Don't get mad, I didn't understand but, I now know I do
Everyone that I think I love may not love me too. She may not be
     you.
I was careful; I thought I had found the one, my sun.
I knew my stay in heaven had begun, but now I gotta run.

It takes two to make it through. I was counting on you.
I can forget that too
So I'll do what I must do, there's no more me and you
I'll have to forget about that too, I'll forget about you.

# Gone To Stay

I've come up hard from the start as a juvie my life was dark, I born into nothing wanting something my FAM thought I was heading for trouble. Seeing riots and violence my confusion was doubled, Mama Dea died before I was seven, my grandma left me before I was eleven; my real mama was always sending me away. Six-trey was so jacked I couldn't even go out to play. I lived my life as a teen waiting on judgment day there was always some roadblock in my way some authority figure that didn't want to listen to what I had to say. I don't know about you but to do this again ain't no way. I'm all grown now I still wanna play but my child hood is gone, and it's gone to stay.

I hit the ground running from birth I never learned how to pretend. That same shit I ran from I keep seeing again but haters and smoked out freaks turn my gains into sin, now the air is thin. I don't care about the mass's I just don't want to move back again. I'm dodging mental lapses; ain't no groundhog day my friend. Ain't no friend in the end I can't shake my sins. Father Leary told me to learn to chill just be real you'll see the rest of the world is in it for the thrill, or just against a positive will. He was my only friend but my Fam thought I was gay. Once again my mother sent my confused ass away now I'm living that same hurt again it's just another mother fucking day. My child hood is gone and it's gone to stay.

I'm all grown now alone now but surviving pound for pound, I've been knocked around I've been close but I've never hit the ground. I've wanted many things but what I've needed has always been around. Surviving since I was a child never allowed to run wild never allowed to fail out of all the dirt I did only spent eight days in jail. I put PJ through a living hell, so what did she do committed suicide before the age of 22. Depended on me now her life is through, I don't expect you to understand I'm just telling what I've been through, but maybe you can if you were me what would you do. I've had some hard knocks but I ain't trying to die,

I ain't trying to lose I'm a Blackman strong tired of paying dues, tied of being used the most feared mammal on the planet with limited options to choose. So when you see me don't fear me cause I mean no harm to you; just trying to chase the blues away
I'm all grown now thinking about a childhood with no play. But my childhood is gone now and it's gone to stay.

# Good-Bye

I feel your warmth as you lay next to me,
You say you love me, so why are you wrecking me, just checking
    see
Is there no wonder, I did let you get close to me
I thought this was love, as love was suppose to be
Now all I see is you coming back to me, that wont be, you see
Now I'm banking and at peace with me
When you left all my pain and rain ceased to be, I feel free
To explore, I want more then what use to be
I'm now banking and I thank you, for not choosing me

How did we get here where pain and rain are the same?
Where broken hearts, with scars just ain't no thang, change
Is suppose to come just from living, I was living with pain
You made me change, my direction, my affection,
You feel the same as me
In that you wanted us not to be, I feel free
To be the man that I was meant to be, just live, reality
Is life as life is magic, not tragic, or pain over and over again?
And again, just to start and end, again, no one wins
When that love is pain to change, then hurt again, that's a sin

Good-Bye yesterday is a memory long gone
I feel I did no wrong, so Good-Bye
Relieve me of my reasons to cry
Just leave me it seems to me without a try
Good-Bye my love Good-Bye

13

# Hey Black Man.

Hey brother, hey black men tell what in the world are you thinking? Or, are you thinking? Isn't life about more than I, don't we, as black men have the responsibility to help write our history the way we want to be remembered? Or, are you gonna let another dictate to you how your child is to be reared or, how the black woman will rise and be another force that you must deal with in order to survive. I hear you. You think I don't? What I hear are slogans that mean shit. What I hear is how you run this, and that, but can't even run your life. Your females are moving and, they are not waiting. You don't wont to work for $7, 8$ dollars and hour. Your woman will. You won't fall into that B.S. of having to start on the lower level to get to the main floor. Your woman will. Some of my brothers will. But tell me what's your plan? Hip Hop your way to a better life? What kind of life? The very Hip Hop force's that you worship are making dollars and don't give a damn about nothing but concert tickets and CD sells. Even on that level we still find our brothers are still the same. But. I want to get back to my brothers and being black. Being BLACK MEN.

If history has taught us any thing, as a people is that we can over come anything. The hardest things that we've had to overcome our black forefathers have done that. They died so that we can live, walk, and work almost anywhere. They died because they would rather be dead than to live, as they were being force to live. How many people must die in order for you to see that we are, as black men are standing still; and that's just where they, the mass's that are in control want you. A blind man is no threat in a fight even if he has a gun. He may be able to shoot, but at what. We are just that, walking, seeing blind men. Just look at what's happening now.

Get up any morning around 7AM or 8am what do you see?

Your sisters getting up getting the kids ready for the day and getting off to work. And all of them don't have good jobs but have they have jobs.

What do you see when you go to stores or restaurants. Sisters shopping with other sisters, sisters having diner with other sisters, sisters interacting with other sisters, not because they're gay, but, because they share that one thing in common, survival. Where are you?

Don't get me wrong there are some very powerful brothers out there doing for there families, doing in there communities, and just doing the very things that it would take to write a positive history. Yet, for every one we can find there are maybe a dozen that aren't doing squat. Where dose this end my brothers I'll tell you.

Pride. Pride is good to have. Pride will take you places that no other emotion will take you. It's pride that makes you pull a gun a kill some one because he or she dissed you. It's pride that'll make you beat your woman because she's moving in the positive and tells you to get off you ass help the family. It's pride that makes you survive when you in up in jail and realize that it maybe too late. But why wait that long, why wait until you've bottom out. Why? Pride. You'll rather stand tall in another nothing brothers eyes then, to stand tall with your woman, and your family. You'll rather ruin yourself just so you can have your name on a wall in the alley with R.I.P., a monument that no one gives a damn about. Your woman won't bring your child or, children by to see it. She shouldn't. But she may have to because that's the only legacy that's left of you. Pride.

Why can't pride make you take that seemingly nothing high school diploma and go on to somebody's college? Why can't pride make you achieve things that NO ONE can take away? You can still have your cars, your jewelry if you must, or anything else that you want.

A good example professional athletics, well maybe not the best example but the only one we all can relate to at this moment. Some dress and act just like the characters in Hip Hop songs that so many adore. This didn't just start happening back in the day they dress in the so called "pimp outfits".

But, the one thing they did first was "make" a way for them selves. The only one who could take away what they have is "them". That street life B.S. is not long lasting. The police, or, your brothers will take you down and all that you have. You'll still have your pride though. But dead men don't have a need for any. Nobody gives a damn about your pride in the joint. So you say your other brothers are there, we have each other's back. Maybe, I doubt it. You'll be beholden to somebody in the there. One day you'll have to pay that debt. Be it while you'll there or when you get out. If you're strong and, wise enough to get out of paying it, you were that in the beginning only you had to bottom out before you realized it. Why?

Pride is a dangerous thing unchecked. However, if we don't have a family structure to build upon, to teach our young black men how to be men where do we start? Sisters are teaching their daughters how to be strong sisters when they grow up. No fault of the sisters, and nothing against them for trying but, how can she teach your son how to be a black man, let along a man. She can teach him her version, she can teach him what she wish's a man in her life would be like. Then, you have a confused young man that is easily tempted by misguided PRIDE. Do you think that if your son saw you go off to work everyday he'd just hang around with his buddies be a bailer or whatever else the streets led him to. Maybe. But, that's where you come in. That's what your legacy will be about to see that it doesn't happen to him. Sure, sometimes after all your gallant efforts he still may be what he is. Your fault, maybe, did you try, were you there? If yes is the answer then you did your part, you did what was required of you as a man to be there for your children and start them on the right road.

Whether they travel that path of perceived righteousness or not is in the hands of the one you choose to call God and, that young man. You greatly improve your chances of having your children break that generation after generation of life long poverty and jobs.

You see whoever said it first was right. "A job ain't nothing but work" and, who wants to work all they're lives.

**990829AMS**

IV

# I Keep Trying

My pain magnified by the strain of protecting my gains, I'm living change, just giving
I'm numb to the shame, I'm glad you came. You kept smiling and came back again.
Set my life off with a kiss six weeks later you got me dodging a twist, what part of having my back is this? Skimming twenties and tens, got your ex in my whip, two others fools beefing I'm reaching for my clip. But they were cool didn't want beef from a brother; we realize this sister just has us up against one another. We're better than that, we're brothers in the same struggle being born black.

Why do I have to die to feel peace, why do I have to cry for you to notice me
Why do I have to ask why, I keep trying
Learn to live with the backstabbing and lying, I keep trying
I don't expect much we're just living and dying; I keep trying
I keep trying, no time for crying I keep trying

I'm trying hard to maintain I feel like exploding, like life is eroding, you look at me you think I'm joking, with no eyes on me I'm smoking, Shantes calling but I'm not going. This dramas broken down like my life's story. Tearnee and sometimes Tory, look at the price I pay for a little bit of glory. Quick hits doing that eight-mile trick weather your own storm but you got your own click needing more but this is all I get, to proud to quit.
Sometimes I feel like a target waiting to be hit. But Layton tells me we gotta stick, you want proof I'll give you fact. The masses couldn't last a day if any of them were born black.

Why do I have to die to feel peace, why do I have to cry for you to notice me
Why do I have to ask why, I keep trying
Learn to live with the backstabbing and lying, I keep trying
I don't expect much we're just living and dying; I keep trying

I keep trying, no time for crying I keep trying

Within my mind into a place I find, within this space is time; it's so unkind. So I reach for a tastes of black label with a Moet chase. Moving at my own pace so don't hate, I'm just me and I like spending cake or is that cheddar, whatever. I'm in my own zone and I feel together or just blunted, keeping it real never fronting, I'm just wanting no drama
I apologize cause this ain't what I promise, I didn't make a difference in your life and that goes out to my mama. Chill when there's no thrill cause sex was stormy, but this is real life I can't stop I'm still going, thirsting for the knowledge of the knowing, I was born black so I keep my shit flowing.

Why do I have to die to feel peace, why do I have to cry for you to notice me
Why do I have to ask why, I keep trying
Learn to live with the backstabbing and lying, I keep trying
I don't expect much we're just living and dying; I keep trying
I keep trying, no time for crying I keep trying

# I Want You With Me

It's magic when you speak my name, you're a habit I'm reluctant
    to change
You're my sunshine, I feel me needing you,
I spend my time cause I always wanting to
Be with you, just do what you do, I want to be the man that you
    turn to
For conversatin or dating,
It's really all up to you,
I'll be waiting. My life is about you
I get this thrill when you're touching me,
I get a chill when you're loving me,
I see a us as in we're a pair, I see you and me cause
I know you care, so let's share
This life and all it's ecstasies, be my wife I'll give you the best of
me, is that something that you can see, so take my hand I want
you with me

That's all that I can see, my life has you with me,
That's how my life should be
I want you with me. I want you with me.
That's seems to be the best for me, live this dream of you and me,
    I do
I want you with me. I want you with me.

There was no way for me to pass you by.  That smile.
Those eyes, I just loved your style
I just love the way you say my name, this is not a game,
I want to share my everything.
I want to give you what others never get to,
I want to name an island after you
Most of all I love that desire in you that fire in you.
Can I be the man for you?
Let's enjoy hard times no more, nothing's gonna be like it was
    before, never gonna hurt anymore, for sure.

Be my wife for life, how about a 10 karat piece of ice, nice
How about it being you and I for life?  How about it being we?
So is this something that you can see, if you can take my hand
I want you with me.

# It's On

Sometimes I feel I don't belong, it's on brothers acting like hoes, out of check it shows now you fucking with my flow. I ain't into checking, this shit be how it goes, who knows. Ain't no right or wrong, in this shit I don't belong, I'm looking at the bitch in you I'm out of here I'm gone.

I'm still a man I have nothing to prove to you, I wanna be free and that has nothing to do with you, I got no beef unless you refuse to give me peace, so can I break, or what you wanna do, peace to you I'm on a mission with vision it's one plus two, I'll pull through, it's me with Crystal in black, I like her like that. Pretty face thought she had my back, turn around is fair play but how many times is that, this click is whacked. You think I'm some other dude better check your facts.

Its on, tonight's my night you better leave me alone, I'm rolling strong
It's on, this click feels right nobody has to die tonight I'm rolling strong
I'm rolling strong

This ain't misery even though I'm unhappy most times, Layton taught me to respect myself so I'll be fine, this is my space my time sometimes the loose is tight but I keep my mind, spend 3 Bens on a Dyme, turn out just a waste of time, but it was fun and that's enough, making it when times are rough, surviving just to get enough, I'm not a bad man but my heart is tough

I come up hard Chi Town action I learned my lines and played my part, street life is behind me but life reminds me of the me I once knew, the me that was trying sometimes crying just for a few, I'm not missing this world I feel this is my queue, my do so stop pushing me fool your B S is B S and that ain't cool just bullshit dude.

# Just Tricking

I saw you standing; I'm glaring, just staring
I've already moved past your name
For me it's a beginning, if I'm winning, I'll be sinning
You like me best be thinking about this game
With some help I take my step, I play my ace first
I'm going all out, no doubt, this is my chance
Quick as a blink, I think, is this better or worse, a curse
If I land her, can I stand her, it's all romance

I'll be just tricking

It's all about cop and blow, for show, I'm just hitting
If I were you, you'd be me, you'd see, I ain't about quitting
This ain't no love, because, it was you being foolish
Wanna be a lover, undercover, what kind of drugs you using
You be gagged and bound, tied down, out of circulation
I see you wishing, cause you missing, all this sex-u-lation
In the end, I try and pretend, that I ain't never lonely
It ain't easy but it's pleasing, forsaking love for sex only

I'll be just tricking

# Keep Your Shit Together

What kind of life Layton are you living when you can curse the very god that life is giving, there's so much pain with every breath you breath you wanna go but you're just to afraid to leave. Don't be naive; you just don't want to be the reason to make Thelma grieve. So I face the challenges of being a man and all that then multiply by ten and add in you're black. This drives me crazy cause it doesn't have to be, now I must face a new reality some things just are cause that's how shit be. I see myself outside of who I am I've tried so much do I really give a damn or am I afraid that I may lose, I'm just tired of having to pay more dues.

Layton I understand you're not in this alone; God is here he's never left you on your own. Life is a struggle from shit to sacrifice you can't take no more, to quit is to give up on life. I love you man you got to play this out, turn the page see what tomorrow is all about. Then push on keep moving on; now turn another page I can forgive you if you die of old age. But nothing else for you so what are you gonna do. Be a man or bitch up and say you're through if for no one else you must be true to yourself, or are you afraid to loose. I'm just tired of paying more dues.

Eternal life is yours if you can hold it together; you paid the ultimate sacrifice you could have earned forever.
But because you didn't believe you get never. Eternal life is for those who can keep their shit together. Our time is now not whenever; our time is now so keep you shit together.

I can take the static turn the page sometimes-good shit happens, it's just a balance in life no one wins all the time. But each win comes at a price that we must pay usually like a layaway. Pay a little bit every few days just like always here comes change severe and unexplained takes away your smiles instantly with pain. Hurricane type rain; feeling so low you've forgotten about all your gains what's up Layton you can't take a little strain. I know you can take this in stride keep you shit alive and keep riding high. Keep carving up that I made it up that I made it out of the hood pie, this rags to riches blessing a keep living lesson, so what's up Layton just checking.

Eternal life is yours if you can hold it together; you paid the ultimate sacrifice you could have earned forever.
But because you didn't believe you get never. Eternal life is for those who can keep their shit together. Our time is now not whenever; our time is now so keep you shit together.

# Let Me Be The One

Let me be the one to hold you, console you, just let me love you
I wanna be the one you know that loves you
Anytime that I am near you, it's clear to you, just let me hear you
Tell me that you know it's me who loves you
Just let me be the one who knows you love him
Just let me be the one

I can't help it, you've touched me, you've never laid a hand on me
But I feel you, It's real to me, and you don't even know it's me
That needs you, believes in you, and you think that I'm just being
    a friend
But you're special, I'm careful, not to ever let our friendship end

Am I wrong, am I alone, in wanting this and you for my life
I would lie for you, I'd try for you, to be your husband, will you
    be my wife
I'd do for you, I'd be true to you, you can respect and expect that
    I'm here for you
There's no danger, or anger, my love is love just know that
I'd be there for you

# Live us Again

I bruised you, abuse you, I guess I misused you,
No respect for myself let alone for you
But through all this, with just a kiss, some bliss,
It seemed that pain did not exists
But it did, cause I did to you, so wrong I was to you,
I cry, because I do love you
I was wrong ain't no doubt about it,
I'm not bragging I'm not proud about it
I was blessed to have known you then,
I just wish it was a us again, an again
I just wish that I could live us again.
I just wish I could live us again


So I lost your body but not your heart,
I broke my own right from the start
Of the grabbing and shouting aloud,
The accusing an abusing but now
I blame others, lovers, even you,
For making me act the way that I do
I was wrong ain't no way around it
Lost in a sea of doubt, I tried to drown it
Now I see I was blessed to have known you then,
I just wish it was a us again, an again
I just wish that I could live us again.
I just wish I could live us again

# Welcome To My Life

Welcome to my life, My Life, this is My Life
Welcome to My Life, (My Life)

Late at night I scheme while most peeps dream, I lived my life this way, 40 years and a day, I was free
I could have been locked away, all work never learn how to play, never learned how to make life pay
I ain't sad I was brought up that way, Doing and using just choosing not to be losing, Life is confusing
What worked for him may not work for them, it was okay for you but for me that wont do, it's true
I should be saying thank you, I learned early on to be strong, learned to get alone, learn to get it on
You strike I gotta strike back, it's like that being born black, just facts, but I wouldn't change a thing
I'm a man that's born of kings and queens' diamond mines not just diamond rings, but now I dodge gangs
And the trouble the street brings, everything seems different everything seems the same

Welcome to my life, My Life, this is My Life
Welcome to My Life, (My Life)

I was brought up in Woodlawn on 63$^{rd}$ street, Disciples and Blackstone Rangers, male and female freaks
Veronique was a treat that taught me to ____ should have heeded the lesson but I was hooked, boiling water
I learned how to cook, every penny I had brother Kenny took, but that's my fought, I was caught by a
Trap set by my self, turn my back on Denise I thought I didn't need anyone else, but Rell saved me from that
Demon I call real life, I repaid her by making her my wife, and then ex-wife number two, a fool once will
Be a fool cause that's what fools do, is that true? I had to pass cause I told a many people fuck you

28

And all that drama that you do if you don't understand the plan
I'm the man to put that shit in hand, but I was
Wrong just being big and strong, one day that strength will be
gone then it's my turn to burn but before then
I'll learn how to turn, and earn the trust of one, will you be the
mother of my son, before life is done?
I need to know that I was right with you, I miss you Thelma
there'll never be another you, (I love you)

Welcome to my life, My Life, this is My Life
Welcome to My Life, (My Life)

All that stressing was a blessing, taught me a lesson, I moved up
out the hood I changed my zip code but
Some of these motherfuckas ain't no good, or just abortions that
didn't work, spreading drama spreading
Hurt, 2001 racism still exist I can make all the money you want
but peace of mind ain't on your list, ain't no
Need for this, all I want is peace with this life, one day that'll turn
into two guess that's two to many change
Another law is what you do, just to benefit you, guess you forgot
that a black man has needs too

Welcome to my life, My Life, this is My Life
Welcome to My Life, (My Life)

# Night Life

Maybe we will again, make love again, no, okay
No more again, guess I can save that sin
As we try to live this life, others always try
To see us die, force us to sacrifice, some life
But if we live in days gone by, we'll always find
That we're always dying, and still we're trying
To find our wisdom, we don't listen
You like me finally see
We're caught up, brought up for that
Night Life, where living feels so right, there's no limit til sunlight
In the, Night Life


Hold on; never mind that bullshit about being free
Those words don't seem to apply to me
Can't drive my ride or I'm DWB
Cause my color is all that you can see
I'm led to believe in the home of the brave
To me the brave was brought in as a slave
In the work place I chase that same dream
Then I'm told that this job is not what I need
You like me can finally see
We caught up, brought up for that
Night Life, we're living it all night, doing life just right
In the Night Life

# No Glory

No early rising just visualizing my day, looking for any surprises, fake fools in disguises
Rapping and acting like they're my friends, just grinning and pretending, steady spending
My ends, but then again I guess that makes me the fool for choosing a friend such as you
For wanting to, just believe in you. Sometimes hope should be a sin. You didn't let me down I found, I wanted you around. I just like the way it was me and you. I like the play
And the ways you say you do. That's always gonna be between me and you. You're the
Mother of the child that I wish I knew, It was not for me not wanting to, She doesn't
Understand so why should you. So what's up Shonte or should I say hommie',
Still keeping to yourself or just from me only, this is my song this is my story, no glory

This should be magic, but to live is tragic so much drama happens no reason, drunk luck
Or plucked from your dreams far to soon, live your life with fear of doom, in fear of fear
Afraid of everything because nothing is clear, just the tragedies on the news, we chose to
Be confuse, for fear blinds our sight, gotta be but how can this be a grandfather before
I'm forty, 2 mothers one son, one daughter, I drowning, you hand me water
Or maybe its me who sees night racing into day, as we scrambling meaninglessly
On our way, live and play settle up is this judgment day, phone rings another bill I don't
Wanna pay. But I pay to play. Shonte tell what did my son say or was that Spring and Toni. All my nights feel like days I can't sleep anyway, I can't think during the day

Same song hums along, like a lesson learned poorly, this is my story, no glory

Just like life flips those lessons don't spend your life second guessing just be who you
Know to be not what you think others will see which bring me to me, back to this fantasy
Call life with me, burning greens and spending endlessly, when you left me I was doubting me, blaming me, blaming everything that came into contact with me. I'm sorry
Traci, you really meant a lot to me. And RC, I wish that there was never a me and you
It took me two years just to move past you, I was a fool when we first spoke I should have hung up on you, but through it all I did learn from you, I wish the best for you,
Bye Boo. Me too. Now I have my K-Day to brighten my path, someone who I wish to share what I have, a smile, a laugh. A step away from my past, a new way to play
My sunshine my K-Day, there's a smile in every grin, every heartache ain't no sin
Be true to yourself, never give in to the hype, this is life, this you and me homie
This is my song sing along a lesson one of many; this is my story, no glory

# One Time To Win

I tried change this fake world where everybody's about game, every new
Face brings about strain, the silence of violence brings about quick pain, so
Keep strangers at arms length you control the flame, never play another's mans
Game you got one shot at this you can't come back again
One shot, one time to win

## ONE TIME TO WIN

For show ain't no rewind or return to go so don't act surprise like you didn't know
Crying tears from dry eyes, telling true lies backed by false alibi lies, I hear the Shallow cries now I see your fears, I've lived them for years, now I see your tears
Now I see them clear you can't come back again, one shot one time to win

## ONE TIME TO WIN

At one point I lost control I reached for hope I got fake gold sex with no soul
Nothing but drama so I chose drugs I learned to roll. Thought I was the shit
But my life was on hold I looked for answers I don't like this hand I'll fold
Back up this is my life let me grab a hold you got one shot at this you can't
Come back again, one shot one time to win

## ONE TIME TO WIN

What kind of world is this where adults believe in make a wish, your ten year old

Son already has had his first kiss nephews older than uncles that's
just another
Twist no family structure is what we're up against, more fake
prophets but even
More bullshit, you got one shot at this you can't come back again,
one shot one time to win

# ONE TIME TO WIN

My lives exposed with each track I bring what's in my heart the
thought in my Brain, my life's drama it's ups and change a lot of
shit can hurt but don't mean a Thang, there's a little bit of sun in
everything haters and leeches remind me that There's still strain,
can never relax being black in this game you got one shot at this
You can't come back again, one shot one time to win

# ONE TIME TO WIN

# Playing The Game

I often hear people refer to everything as "game". As in sporting game, shooting game, game on, game off, game being shot down. I understand fully, do you?

I often hear people say that if you don't have game you can't play. I thought I had game, so I tried to play.

How can you play a game when there are no rules. What, you make them up as you go? I guess so. I thought I had game so I tried to play.

Is having game being cool, or is being cool having game? If there's a difference I thought I knew. I thought I was the rule, not the exception. I thought I had game. So I tried to play.

It use to be cop, block, lock and show, easy come, easy go. But a 3 lettered word put an end to that, in fact threw a curve in the playa's act. Above all else I kept to myself then along came my queen, now I can be the king. I thought I had game so I tried to play.

Fun nights that lasted weeks long, no matter the beat I was her song. She spread joy without a try, for me the perfect woman had just stop by. But before I said what is a game with no rules, it's just a foolish sport played by fools. I thought I had game so I tried to play.

I often hear people say that they got game, they control this and that, that they are in her head. Thinking that I'm all that I tried to lead and was led. I had the perfect woman in the palm of my hand, nothing that I did she just like me the way I use to be. I use to show her love at every turn, I listen to that game and I was the one to get burn. I thought I had game so I tried to play.

I'm not one to preach, a physic, or any of that. I just know, I lost the one flower in my world that I could love, and over time would blossom and grow. Maybe game works for some but I don't believe that. I don't believe that concept for it's a selfish and foolish act. So you say that I'm just mad cause my game was weak, I let a cherry come and knock me down have me stumbling on my feet. I guess you're right, no, I know that you are. Not because I couldn't play, but because I listen to you. And I don't even know who you are. Someone said don't hate the playa hate the game, a wiser man once said to thy own self be true. If I had listen to him maybe my lady wouldn't have come to me and said baby we're through. For you started out a man, now I don't know what a have, if you want to play some kind of game I'm a woman you're no longer in my plan. So to all you playa's playing a game that has no rules, every playa will get played, for every fool will be fooled. I thought I had game so I tried to play.  990830AMS

VI

# A Product of the Streets

Everybody's got a story this is just a small part of mine.

I was born on judgment day, I was born to live and die this way
I ain't go stray, I wouldn't change a thing, I enjoy the sunshine
I'll endure the rain and pain, cause I'm a product of the streets
I'm everyday people; from six-tre mean beats don't feel no heat
I'm everyday people I'm a product of the streets

I travel strong bad boys work alone, need no witness's
I do my do and be gone, but I've known men that were bitches
Straight snitches, as strong as they wanna be but everybody's got
a weakness
This one was madness from one-shot gladness; she tipped the
scale at 8 of 10
Pretty face, very soft skin, I almost changed my program now
that would be a sin with no forgiveness to give this street life is my
hustle this is how I live

I wont complain cause that a bitch thang, men should never show
their weakness
Being jealous that's what hoes do, how you gonna run with a crew
and be envious
Over another mans click, get the fuck out me face with that weak
ass shit, you bitch
Ain't no room for that on this trip, you ain't worth a needle
That final trip in a black tuxedo, no thank you I'll pass
I don't even want a bitch nigga to kiss my ass

I live the game lived a life engulfed by flame, living a life
That should never be tamed that should never be changed, my
gains in life came from pain, I'm drenched ain't no shelter from
the rain, so I learn to live with pain

**Fuck you this is my life and I don't believe in shame cause if you could you'd do the same, we call life that but this shit ain't no game life on the six tre taught me how to make life gain for me this life style ain't no thang for me this is me and this is how I'm gonna be**

# A Street Called Life

I've tapped out, mapped out, survived, and sacrificed
I'm just riding down a street called life
Complicated, but situated, fine print never stipulated
Have to pay just to be, life's not free, living to be hated
Spoken words claim of being free, I'm waiting, still chasing
That dream, some scheme, in fact we're always hesitating
Funny thing is, none of this seems real, til we grieve
Pain we feel, that rain is real, our shadow as long as we live
I'm cruising with this bruising, seems I'm steady using
Sometimes losing, these one-way streets I'm choosing
Trying to make things right, I'm riding down a street called life
Riding down a street called life

Another page turned, a lesson learned, yeah right, I don't think so
It's a show, a hit of blow, now tell me which way to go
Follow you no way, I'm lost enough all by myself
Felling like I'm needing another, a lover, alone I need someone
   else
I've had lovers, a wife, my mother, my brother, and some trouble
Tried thinking, then drinking, saw all my troubles double
At a fever pitch, I found my niche was here, within myself
With my god, a job, and my daughter, I'm not needing anyone
   else
I'm still cruising, I learned from my bruising, stop using
Stop losing, oh yeah, some better friends I'm now choosing
Just trying to make things right, I'm riding down a street called
   life
Riding down a street called life

# The Fly

I got no complaints but I can't take the restraints, my suggestion
But I'm guessing when I say I'll play but I can't keep playing this
    way.
I'm in danger, I feel anger a burning rage inside, I hate I know
    you lied
But that's just human nature, even of that, I'm not sure. I endure
I don't seek a cure. I can solve this. Make a wish. This is the real
World now peep this. A problem I'll solve them got no time for
    revolving
On that bull that has been called the truth, need more proof
How about being about making dollars all rollers ain't ballers

Living this Life, and I'm living it on the fly, on the fly

(MOSTICKS)
I'm the stick man, the hit man the good as you get man who can
Put you in the mood to smooth your soul, lose control, and grab a
    hold
I'm here to clear your thoughts of pain; no rain second coming is
    here again
Understand, I'm not them, I'm the man, never forget my plan,
    Black as
You get again; never losing to chicks again, last sin when a win is
    a win
Now I'll begin, I'm making monies; sexing honies this life is no sin
But think again all that glimmers, is really grimmer to blind to
    see, living
A life that's really living me, a fantasy, pure ecstasy, Take a little
    ride
And spend some time with me.

Living this Life, and I'm living it on the fly, on the fly

I had to back up or get jacked up I'm always watching my back,
    just facts

But the truth is what you believe in not what you're seeing I'm
the beginning

I see you grinning, peep the game that I'm spinning, you feel like
sinning

Maybe some wine then dine, romantic music just spending time. I
wanna talk

To you be a part of you walk with you touch the very heart of
you, us two

Is that something that you can do? How about a cruise for two,
just me and you.

Living this Life, and I'm living it on the fly, on the fly

(FEMALE)

You talk that smooth hit, pure player kick, is that suppose to
stick, not here

You ain't even near a chance, this ain't about romance not yet,
let's dance

I wanna know more about you, what's inside what you like to do,
the real you

The you that not many see, the sensitive side that you hide trying
to hard to be

Like you're thought to be. Not taught to be. I need to see you for
me, you see

If time is all that you need, then come spend some time with me

Living this Life, and I'm living it on the fly, on the fly

I always thought that time was for play, until those I knew went a
way to stay

No time to waste on game play, leeches, skeezie chicks that trick
for pay, go away

Be my friend now, and in the end you'll stay, But then again, the
end is the end

No need to pretend. No need to try again, same sign same sin, no
one can win

The prize was in knowing you, the dream was to love you, just
whole you

Pave the way in gold for you, I'd damn near sell my sold for you,
    Okay
Maybe we can be fly away, to our hide away, our own special
    place, love me
Face to face, any kind of pace, sit back and share a taste.

Living this Life, and I'm living it on the fly, on the fly

# The Same Lie

I can't believe this shit. It's tragic, 2001 this racism kick still
    happens
It's madding. That I have to change to be accepted,
I can't be me I have to be what you expected, or I'm rejected.
Keep a brother guessing. I can't be black no more.
Determined that I rise no more, Hate is your favorite lesson.
I'm a child of god I still receive my blessing. For What,
All that bullshit that you put me through now equals nothing
I ain't a criminal, I got you paying me don't that tell you
    something.

Now peep this, I want you to keep this. We're many of one,
And that's our uniqueness. Street ness. But we're envious,
And greedy, that's a bad combination when you realize,
That we're also the needy, so visualize in your mind,
The prize. A world where you can be you and not be penalized,
I can't, there's something in my eyes. Racism, Placsim,
One after another we keep living that same lie, until we die
Now tell me where's the peace in this, cause this shit still exist
So many groups still resists, us as a people, Blacks still not equal
With no black men you'll have no sequel, what's that you say
One Race. One God. One People.

# Things You Can't See

Since I've been around from Chi-Town, I've found life is so much different from then to now. There's no returning to that magic this is a new day with new happenings, different friends but there's still back stabbings, I can feel the peeps laughing but it's not me I'm not the clown it's just ghetto tragic that's how clicks be when you believe in things that you can't see.

I was born of Thelma, born in Selma, that's Alabama, the heart of Dixie it taught me quickly, trust in self I felt the world was against me whenever I trusted anyone else. Force to pledge allegiance in the colored school no choice but to grow up swiftly and live by but one rule. Life was nothing nice in fact life was very rude, I bounce from one home to another, one day of peace was followed by many of trouble, never knew my real father and now he's deceased one life so many dreams one life by any means, dropped dollars on a scheme just another busted bubbled. Soap opera fantasy this life is a cold reality, but that just how life be when you believe in things that you can't see.

I went from drinking to smoking to snorting to not thinking pupils dilated not even blinking. Then came two years I wish I could take back, with due fears a life of crack, street life consume me I was young gifted and black, it was like that but I overcame; of that I'm proud, of my life is no shame I survived I'm a true graduate of that game, survived the pain and strain on living a life consumed by that flame, I'm older now and I'll never go back again but everyday of life brings about a new kind of change. Life is just problematic every good one brings another day of static, it's true sometimes shit just happens it's true life is magic. No one convinced me it just made sense to me the life I've lived was just meant to be, I was born in a world that never wanted me, lied to me told me that I was free, now I have to wait for the sequel I am a black man will I ever be equal, not as long as I commit genocide, using or selling then trying to hide I know this is redundant but I'm a black man and I have to much pride. Soap opera fantasy this life is a cold reality but that's just how life be when you believe in things that you can't see.

# Together

You do for me I'll do for you, we can grow to forever, no matter the weather, we don't care about never, because we'll be Together, Together

Keep your mind right life will be tight, I got your back and it's like I'll help you get to that light, don't worry about wrong with me everything will be alright, everyday can be like last night, I'm not just showing force I'm welding might, that's right
We're two that belong, you be me I be you and it's on, peep the magic of a relationship that strong, you feel now cause we be on, this click is strong. Ain't no losing, abusing none of that midnight confusion, I see you like the rhythm that I'm choosing the way I'm moving, so I'll keep on doing what I'm doing, this ain't about using—we're Together

You do for me I'll do for you, we can grow to forever, no matter the weather, we don't care about never, because we'll be Together, Together

Just a brief time to live an laugh, no matter how much just enjoy what you have, this time is to short as time will past, I may not have been your first but I wanna be your last I wanna be the best of everything that you've ever had the reason you don't have to feel hurt or sad I know it's just a title but I'll be your man. It's you and me in all my plans. I'm bringing the best I got to give you all you can stand. I wanna hear you say I'm the man weather we're walking or talking, sexing or just necking I want you to know I can, just checking.

You do for me I'll do for you, we can grow to forever, no matter the weather, we don't care about never, because we'll be Together, Together

# Watch Your Assz

Now it's summer time brothers peeping others at the spots
Some others be tipping but you ain't taking what I got
To some it's very easy laying low deep in some cut
Waiting for a moment of weakness, then he'll tip up
Say brake yourself or I'll be taking a life, think to yourself
About your family, you think back on your life
Now it's in the hands of some other man, no plan
Just want quick cash for his other hand
Give me your keys and cash and I'll let you live
You ain't hearing that, in this junky you don't believe
While you're hesitating he's getting shaky then panics
Then you brace yourself you wait but nothing happens
With no lead for his gat he has to break out running
Now you're gunning but you let it pass
Lesson learn your life could get burn if you don't watch your assz

## If you don't Watch Your Assz, Watch Your Assz

Just cursing summer breeze flowing your ride is dust free
Just thinking how nice it would feel with a brand new lady
You have a woman in your corner but she lacks that bedroom
  action
You've made up you mind you want some satisfaction
You see a pair of jeans that are packing, attacking just attracting
Calling your name so you take the bait and jump into action
In no time you two are a pair, if you see her, you can bet you'll be
  there
You follow her everywhere; your minds in LaLa land somewhere
You don't recognize you've jeopardized your very existence
Everyone that has tried to help have been met with resistance,
  now listen
You ignored the final warning and you job let you go, that ho'
Was gone before you got home because you ain't got no more

You dissed a beautiful woman for some ass and some fun, a little
    sun
But that woman left you with nothing now you're back at one
You don't deserve this but one you dissed wants you to have this
It's a key to her pad, the one you once had, you can come home if
    you wish
You're lucky; I'd leave you out here on your last
Lesson learn your life could get burn if you don't watch your assz
    If you don't Watch Your Assz, Watch Your Assz

# Sitting Back Watching Time

Sometimes I cry, I don't know why
I doubt myself, I wanna be someone else
I don't like what I see, I don't like me
I'll change again, and wreck myself
I'm left to myself again, again, again

I'm, Sitting Back Watching Time……………

I see a light; I feel pain, no sound just rain
I show hate, but fate says your life will change
Life was cold, fun put on hold, true lies told
To death ears, cause life's fears, are about to be true
It's up to you, live or die stand tall or cry
Truth be told, I'm good as gold, in the end we all die

I'm, Sitting Back Watching Time……………

I'm just guessing, this is my blessing, a lesson
In life I want peace, you want me to sacrifice,
My life, I want to live, I wanna be there for my daughter
I want her to live proud, be proud of the things I taught her
Not bought her, not that it matters, time gathers
As shit happens, I'm laughing cuz I can't do this again

I'm, Sitting Back Watching Time……………

# Some People

I refuse to praise or paraphrase recite quotes from folks from my school days I remember people trying to convince me to change my ways believe that life was like Leave It To Beaver or Happy Days. Someone was always telling me that crime never pays, I refuse to believe them I swore that I'd never change, the street life wasn't my enemy I was married to that game. I remember Jimmy and cruising to purple haze, being blunted or froze my life was like a maze. Someone was always showing me evil it was like that dealing with some people, some people.

So I stayed in school, lived by civilized rules but ain't no rules really in this game of life, no collecting two hundred dollars or that perfect wife every revolution of the clock is called age, in life any day could be your last page. I was blinded by lust followed by rage, now it's a eight mile rush I'm watching center stage, but that's just another hell I found myself buying ponytails and press on nails, I was even called late one night to post someone bail, I was free but my mental me was in jail. Even now someone is always showing me evil, life is like that dealing with some people, some people.

I remember stepping to a lady in pink, this woman dissed me without a blink, I was just saying hello and that I saw you earlier today, she said I know you did and moved along her way. Flip as she wanna be, lip that didn't have to be everyone I step to I know is not gonna wanna be with me. But what happen to letting a person down easily, I know a no when it's brought to me. That's just life and there's no recipe for kindness amongst ourselves, for kindness is a weakness that some see as a invitation, many without hesitation to take what you got, so we gotta be hard or that shit wont stop. There's street in all of us and we know that hell is hot, but this ain't Dodge City, I know the weak gets no pity, you stand for yours or your life will be shity living is this land of good and plenty, milk and honey, wanting silk living for money, it's funny. You want it, makes sense don't it. The things we do for self most of the time we're for our own fuck everybody else, so what's left. It's jacked up how some of us are always showing evil, life is like that dealing with some people, some people.

# I Feel So Along

Mama I feel so along now, It's no use to pretend, I spent so much time alone I never let love in, I just need a friend, Mama I feel so along now I don't think I can do this again, I just need a friend, But Mama I feel so along now I can't pretend, I'm grown now I can't do this again, I feel so along now, I feel so along

This price I pay for life, one child two ex wives that move past me to get on with their lives, take this madness is stride can't quit to much pride. I now realize that the ups are the ground, I'm free but my hands are bound bless be the ties that but that life is over now. Praying to a God that is never around. But he knows my stress and strain question him not but I'm so tired of the pain that mental sadness that comes from gains. This life style being weeded and things no one in my corner the price of life in this game.

Mama I feel so along now, It's no use to pretend, I spent so much time alone I never let love in, I just need a friend, Mama I feel so along now I don't think I can do this again, I just need a friend, But Mama I feel so along now I can't pretend, I'm grown now I can't do this again, I feel so along now, I feel so along

I wasn't born in this game I choose to, to do the things I do I'm a hustler but I'm about making ends, I live the life others dream and pretend about, everyone that ever love me I drove out, so this is the fruit of that life. Like always never afraid to pay the price but this feels like twice. It's not about sex I don't wanna be along anymore, I got loot Armani Suits a Gulf stream jet, flying to Vegas dropping million dollar bets I'm looking for stability this life to be reality. I want more than checks and this life style of being weeded and things. I need a different flower is this the price of life in this game.

Mama I feel so along now, It's no use to pretend, I spent so much time alone I never let love in, I just need a friend, Mama I feel so

along now I don't think I can do this again, I just need a friend,
But Mama I feel so along now I can't pretend, I'm grown now I
can't do this again, I feel so along now, I feel so along

# I Lust For Peace Black

I lust for peace black, being me I trust what I see and call it fact; I'm down like that
Last man standing maybe the virgin in the back, another sinkhole; another trap
Another brother grabbing his gat, I lust for peace black I gotta get away from that

You don't see my pain, you can't get by hating my gains I'm a man so I protect my thangs. Waking up getting weeded to get on my way, bracing myself for the games people play. Can you believe this the world is praying to Jesus, why must I die just to feel peace, Death seems like just being deceased, look at the anguish that death brings to a family, struggling with a loss and a new reality. Finance's and expenses, dealing with the Fam that's numb on the senses. This day-to-day shit is relentless I'm being redundant here this life style is just plain senseless.


I lust for peace black, being me I trust what I see and call it fact; I'm down like that
Last man standing maybe the virgin in the back, another sinkhole; another trap
Another brother grabbing his gat, I lust for peace black I gotta get away from that

I'm tired of sister playing the victim, dressing nice but offended cause a brother is looking. Some of us just trying to get with you for a date, but that don't make the next brother fake. Demanding my digits but never phone, give me your number but you're never home. Dealing with me like I'm a prankster, a wanna be gangster. That's why I keep to my on, in my zone I've gotten use to sleeping alone. White girls to smooth my world, Asian girls to give my world a twirl, then there's my Hispanic seniority, what can I say I needed her that's one chapter I'll keep between us. So tell me sisters what part of being my queen is this, I know I'm in this game but what I want dose exist.

I lust for peace black, being me I trust what I see and call it fact
I'm down like that
Last man standing maybe the virgin in the back, another sinkhole; another trap
Another brother grabbing his gat, I lust for peace black I gotta get away from that
I'm Lusting For Peace Black

# Chapter and Verse

Here I go again, chapter and verse

I like pretty faces thick Asses and firm thighs I want a woman that wants a man and not afraid to try no time for the lies and alibis that shit is just a goodbye. In my world that click don't fly beauty is only skin deep it's your mentality that I want to peep, I wanna reach if you can trust me then your trust I'll never breach.

You see
I like what I like born in pain so this rain should be no strain, but it's hard to be what I'll never be again through time my mine and body has changed. But my baby Mary is my burning flame now I forced into a brand new game. Be the lady that feels the same as me, be about making money, wanting to feel that milk and honey, blunted but never wanting having but never needing. Since you're not knowing I'm about showing is seeing the same as believing, I believe in keeping my shit flowing.

Here I go again another chapter and verse, born a black man but that don't mean I'm curse, it was my lifestyle that made my life worse, here I go again through another chapter and verse.

Here I go again another chapter and verse I was born into a racist world that has been filled with hurt, born into a world that believes in self first, here I go again another chapter and final verse.

Since life is all ups and downs I'm living up I know there's a ground, leap of faith I feel gagged and bound, my ships on cruise I haven't reached the ground, I'm still down. So fuck it for I can't live for the masses, closet racist feasting on the have nots I wanna make this turn and struggle not, feel a flame that's red hot. So get your mind right this is me this is what you've got. I face each minute at night, I'm in this twice I'm in this game I didn't know it was for life. It is what it is so let me 'holla'. You'll never need, never grieve all I ask is that you believe, I'll lead but will you follow.

Here I go again another chapter and verse, born a black man but that don't mean I'm curse, it was my lifestyle that made my life worse, here I go again through another chapter and verse.
Here I go again another chapter and verse I was born into a racist world that has been filled with hurt, born into a world that believes in self first, here I go again another chapter and verse.

# No Reason

Is this it my destiny wanted some solitude a little peace of mind, everybody's got drama, attitudes are all I find. Tearany brought peace, Ayanna some grief some relief another twist and turn that's why I burn green-leaf. If I could I would but I can't so I don't think that way I steer clear even though I know crime pays, the risk of time delays. As I grow older stone cold or colder, losing law never knew order. When I broke my jaw you gave me your shoulder. Is it just me or is this shit different now that I'm older.

No reason for the pain, no reason for the change, if I could I wouldn't come back again, no reason to experience this shit again, no reason, when hell is the only season.

My first real experience in life brought me to the altar, it changed my life it was the last thing I needed and I did it twice. I never learned conventional wisdoms, brought up in a fucked up system, street gangs, imitation gold chains, watching Jack and Bill. I'm waiting on Jill or just a woman that can understand how I feel; in the meantime I'm trying to keep my shit real. Missing Tracy and the thrills, Red Lobster or the times we use to just chill, just like yesterday I can't go back again. I'm on a new mission but I don't know where to begin, in another life a win is a sin.

No reason for the pain, no reason for the change, if I could I wouldn't come back again, no reason to experience this shit again, no reason, when hell is the only season

Naked born into strain, makes me never want to come back again. Relive this life again, I got my umbrella but this is more than rain, Woodlawn Gardens or a hustler's game, straight change, deeds done in the dark return as pain. You're living this lie so why look surprised, along in a world I know brothers that kill just to be killing, dealing, and you call this living good times unlisted I took left cause right was twisted. Nine to five was to restrictive, kick game to gain I'm making dollars you can settle for change.

No reason for the pain, no reason for the change, if I could I wouldn't come back again, no reason to experience this shit again, no reason, when hell is the only season
No reason, when hell is the only season.

No reason, when hell is the only season.

No reason, when hell is the only season.

No reason, when hell is the only season.

# Free Your Mind

I learned a lot of lessons that came from a life in the streets, I had
a lot of wins but I learned lessons from my defeats, life is unique. I
was in the fold never sold my soul; I just wanted to rise up that
was my goal. I went from user to producer, neither one was a
joke, I was never use to getting clowned or being broke, for every
frown I just took another pull of smoke. I had to rise up above
that game and put away that yoke.

You See
Free your mind and your ass will follow, this is the real world I
don't have time for sorrow.
Free your mind and your ass will follow, I'm trying to live now I
can't wait for tomorrow. It's time, free your ass and free your
mind, your mind it's time.

I was moving fast no time to think no time to blink, never wanted
to see my last I kept my flame and some Moet to drink; my life
was like the Titanic destine to sink. Never broke, I was grown
only seventeen and hated in the streets, looking for love I had only
my choice of freaks, again there was Veronique. I was living in
overdrive, living large but barely alive; it was 4am when all hell
rushed in. Dropped Ricky and Ken all I saw were flashes of light,
it was four of them, I just knew the Devil had arrived; I was
scared as hell un-hit I survived. But now it's only three of us
where once there were five. This ain't no fable, learn if you want
I'm just putting my shit on the table.

You See
Free your mind and your ass will follow, this is the real world I
don't have time for sorrow.
Free your mind and your ass will follow, I'm trying to live now I
can't wait for tomorrow. It's time, free your ass and free your
mind, your mind it's time.

Living this life is like a alibi sometimes living a lie, a life with no expectations, no reservations, living violence with no hesitations. When you're selling death what do you have left anything else has you second guessing yourself; your every customer is in fact a criminal, maybe your partner is peeping subliminal messages for gains, wanting his own fame. No trusting no one in this game. But you gotta sleep, chill take time to eat it's fucked up when your baby mama is setting you up for defeat. Now you're paranoid, that weed and thangs has your senses devoid of reality. But this is the life you choose so you gotta deal with how shit be, you got paper but your ass is not free, the next crack head could leave you dead but it'll more than likely be your friend, tricking on your ass to avoid the pen. You wanna run but ain't no where to go every new chapter turns out to be like the last episode. Your minds on overload; this drama is an expensive toll on your soul. Now it's just destiny and you I've lived this life so here's my advice to you.

Free your mind and your ass will follow, this is the real world I don't have time for sorrow.
Free your mind and your ass will follow, I'm trying to live now I can't wait for tomorrow.
Free your mind and your ass will follow, spend your time wisely for time you can never borrow
Free your mind and your ass will follow, open your eyes life is the prize
Free your mind and your ass will follow

Can't nobody do it but you

# The Same

When you look the same, things will be the same, things ain't
gonna never change
Your life will remain the same; gains that seem followed by pain
Life won't ever change, when you look the same

I'm living but I don't feel alive, everyday is like Thanksgiving all
because I have a nine to five or is that a one to nine I keep praying
for time, I keep praying for change I keep thinking I'll be fine but
peace like relief seems to be in my mind, or just hard to find,
every new woman wants to keep Layton in a bind. I don't have
time I keep writing instead of fighting, I ain't quitting life feels
freighting. Every time I think I know I find I don't know what
happen you tell me where's the joke I don't feel like laughing. I
don't feel like having another time in my life another wife, my
heart is like butter I see you holding the knife.

When you look the same, things will be the same, things ain't
gonna never change
Your life will remain the same; gains that seem followed by pain
Life won't ever change, when you look the same

This ain't a movie or a script, another sister or brother with lip
I'm a calm but I can make you abandon ship. But that's a
senseless trip; I ain't trying to be the man I'll have to be just to
prove I can't slip. I know everybody standing can get hit, so that's
why I quit. Street-life is built on sacrifice your ass gotta be legit to
stick. I had to change my life that couldn't be as good as it gets?
G's and GD's facing off with V's and Latin C's over keys and all
kinds off twisted shit. Six-Trey violence followed by organ music
and silence I just wanted more than this. Hanging out at Classy
Bee rambling and gambling just trying to see what I could see.
This time I'll paraphrase I wanted to be all I could be, here I go
again I just want to be free. I'm thinking now about Layton I'm
thinking about my mental me.

When you look the same, things will be the same, things ain't gonna never change
Your life will remain the same; gains that seem followed by pain
Life won't ever change, when you look the same

When you look the same, things will be the same, things ain't gonna never change
Your life will remain the same; gains that seem followed by pain
Life won't ever change, when you look the same

# A Night Time Episode

Here I go again, another day I feel my flow no way I know what this day will bring will I suffer or discover, a new enemy or a brand new lover, maybe this time we'll be right for one another. But in the meantime I find I gotta deal with this brother, I apologized but that's as far as I can go. It ain't about right or wrong I just don't want you to wreck my flow. I was hoping he'd just let this shit go, he said no. I'm a grown man so fool I'm not the one I'm a black man and I never learn to run. True to form this fool pull out a gun. I thought quickly this mans someone's brother he's someone's son. I was just kicking it wanting to have some fun. Now it's either a case or a final resting place this fool made me pick one; but I too am a father, a brother and someone's son. I knew this day was trouble before it had begun.

I saw some flashes I said damn something ain't right, I heard some screaming now all I see is light. I heard someone scream another fool got shot tonight. Now there's nothing but silence, the quiet storm of violence, I see faces but they're cloudy, they're not clear. I finally recognize them the faces of the people I shot last year. I see my grandmother telling me to come here, for the first time in my life I feel real fear. This can't be right or is it I feel I'm on display some kind of fucked up exhibit living resistance, a death sentence. I hear Father Leary in the background is it to late for me to listen. I see my grandfather out at the creek fishing, I hear Pastor Terrell preaching about wisdom. I'm walking out in a garden amongst the prettiest shades of green I hear over and over again John 14:13. Then suddenly I hear; my alarm clock ring I'm saying damn this was nothing but a dream.

# I'm Back Again

This is the same old bind, just a different time a different face but the same ole fine. How can I move past this space in my mind constantly with penalties when I've committed no crime; I wanna move forward but I must have hit rewind. Since I'm back here facing mental lapses that come from life's sacrifice's dodging twists with mental devices; no one to lean on so I rely on self starting to cruse God because I've cursed everyone else, this gets worse; turning back to the flame and game cause the straight life hurts.

I'm kissing ass's on the mass's apologizing for doing no wrong a different set of rules when the week are strong. No beats just songs, I don't know the words but I have to sing along. I feel I don't belong in your world and my world has moved on. This ain't no R & B classic but I know this song. Alarm clock rings new day, Still in it I can't play I gotta punch the clock I got monthly bills to pay. My life is living me and I hate living this way. Everyday is different yet everyday feels the same shity way, same shit, different day. Relying on self need is like a vice I got my own fuck everybody else, this gets worse; I'm turning back to the flame and game cause the straight life hurts.

I'm Back Again; I tried change, straight laced and rush hour haste. Got me missing that street game, wanting the relief from that flame.
I'm Back Again; Cause that straight life ain't nothing but pain, nothing but pain.

I hear mama telling me to pray to God and go to church, to me that's just another timed out regime no pay just work. She tells me the rewards are in the here after, to me that's accepting defeat, that's just the final chapter; I can hear my critic's laughter. I could be wrong, but as near as I can tell when you die you're just gone. I wanna live my life now, fuck tomorrow, my 20/20 wont allow. I hear you calling me greedy, fuck that I was born needy. I wanna live my life to the fullest never needing, calm and pleasing. But now all I am is alive, kissing ass's for a nine to five. No one to turn to so I depend on self, I've hard knocked enough fuck everybody else, this gets worse; I'm turning back to the flame and game cause the straight life hurts.

I'm Back Again; I tried change, straight laced and rush hour haste. Got me missing that street game, wanting the relief from that flame.
I'm Back Again; Cause that straight life ain't nothing but pain, nothing but pain.

I'm Back Again

# One Night

I ain't complaining, life has me thinking I can feel me changing, my life rearranging, again. I was brought up to face truth, but I fear no sin but then again. I lust to win, my lust for flesh could be my end. No need to pretend. I want what I want; I wanted you, just not twice. I want to be free yet I wanted you in my life, live nice. Can this be right, this can't be love cause this was just one night; this was just one night.

A selfless love is not the same as being selfish; make a wish, my heart wants more than a kiss. You call my name yet you wont do the same, wont share that flame; all I hear is talk in the game. I do for you; you bring me change, or was that joy and pain, or more of the same. I need not to grieve for the ghost of change. I want the most of this thing called life, live nice. Can this be right, this can't be love cause this was just one night; this was just one night.

Everywhere I go I feel like I'm the show, even when I lay low. Sometimes I feel I can't take anymore, I'm in the game but I don't know the score. You tell me you know how I feel, be real; I'll pay full price cause I don't want a deal. I just want a woman to be real; to lie to me is to treat me like a fool. Liars are destine for fire that's a top ten rule. I just want to maximize this thing called life, live nice. Can this be right, this can't be love cause this was just one night; this was just one night.

# No Place Like Home

The evil I see tells me life will be better in the squeal, my mental me is not free will I ever be equal. I hear the mass's laughing saying this wont be happening, it's maddening. To think of the bigger picture leaves me sadden. Leaves me feeling a life of no hope, so many don't vote, so many roll trees to smoke. I realize it's a sad day when your hope comes from dope. Snorting till I'm broke, doing violence to just to feed my habit and cope. I was hanging myself with my own rope. So I turn to the one I chose to call God, to even the odds learned a valuable lesson from the 'Wizard of Oz'. Learned to leave that trick shit alone, started a family, a foundation, there's really no place like home. Mine was of a single parent by my parent was strong, right or wrong there's no place like home.

Trusting life blindly, being treated by life so unkindly when God calls you home that's finality. Where ever my minds at peace that's where you'll find me. Living inside my own mind because that's where I'm free. Cursing the odds turn my back on God, but that was wrong made my life hard, nothing but trouble my struggle was doubled. Living for flesh another test, you burst my bubble, made my life a fucking mess. My mental me had to get stronger, couldn't settle for less. When more is less or was less more, I can't be more than me, what's this, another test. I really wasn't guilty that's why I didn't confess. I looked for that rainbow but there was no gold, no soul nothing but tricks trying to grab a hold. You knew she was with me that shit was bold. I didn't step out of my role, you let me down and I left you alone. So I keep to my self in my own mind I roam, in real life there's no yellow brick road. But on the forizo there's no place like home.

# Passed Over

Just another chapter, another episode exposed

I know you know the difference between right and wrong, your shit has been one-sided for far to long. I'm told things are better, and on the surface they seem to be the truth is always in the things you can't see but feel, cause the truth be real can't hide your feeling it's exposed in all your dealings, it's just we fight ourselves so much fighting you no one is willing. We just take the chips while you enjoy the cake. You try to show sincerity but we see fake, asses just another day of dealing with the mass's. The sad part is I'm in the front row of this comedy show but I ain't laughing, I'm helping you I'm inhaling gas's. And masking my failures by not having, a family structure, I'm filled with doubt in a life were I'm never sure, like having a disease with no cure. Generations of genocide, a hood life of homicide $200 jumpers worshiping false idols, keep listening to Rev I-know, collection plates and a choir for a show. You keep searching your secret garden for that four-leaf clover; back in the real world we're just getting Passed Over.

I hear you in the back ground talking loud, screaming I'm playing my race card, you made me this way never passive I'm rolling hard. From the start it's been all about race, I know you don't believe me but tell me that face-to-face or better yet just try living in my place. Being qualified but constantly denied then put me at your front door and proclaim diversity with pride, but it's just a lie. But I stand there every day and ask myself why. To let others know anything is possible just don't be afraid to try. Separate but equal one life no sequel, it's only when you suffer drama that we're one people. Your view of curbing drug use is to supply clean needles, what planet are you really from; you wanna curb birth control by supplying condoms. I'm not saying you right or wrong and I'm not backing up this is me and how I feel until I'm gone. Dialing 911 from my home you arrive I have to prove I belong, by then the need for has moved on. Maybe it's me that's looking at the land of the free all wrong. Bet if I spoke with a European accent I'd be rolling strong with help from you, you only talk to me at traffic stops or roadblocks or when my taxes are due. You keep searching your secret garden for that four-leaf clover; back in the real world we're just getting Passed Over.

# This Time

This time this moment right now, I'm doing all right, right now
This feeling' alright right now this moment, this time is now
This moment this time is now

Who's to say so why play the games that we play it's okay to date
but I shy away
I fell in love with Mary and now I write and wait a hell of a fate,
but what's the use in giving chase just to chase, no stamina for
this pace I'm last but not in last place I'm not even in a race, I
don't have rules and this ain't school so love me face to face I
know this to be my fate I take this life in stride and that's day to
day

This time this moment right now, I'm doing all right, right now
This feeling' alright right now this moment, this time is now
This moment this time is now

I'm a member and the president so let me be the man to represent
love sex and sin in your life the reason you wake each day to face
life to help you over come any setbacks or strife, treat you like my
lover and wife all roll into one never being sad EagleOne's ready
to run, we'll dine in Aruba awake Rome, make love in Paris then
dine in a new time zone, so let's not waste a moment cause when
it's gone it's gone no more zooming in a zone let's call now home.

This time this moment right now, I'm doing all right, right now
This feeling' alright right now this moment, this time is now
This moment this time is now

# How Real Is This?

How real is this, life is nothing but a dream, it don't mean a thing, it's nothing but a scheme.

Life is as life is; is priceless, the right stuff makes you want enough survive when times are tough makes you give it up even when you know she ain't worth the fluff. Yet life is as life should be unpredictable and blowing free, plenty trees and leaves to leave your mental being in flowing seas of pain or ecstasy, there's always reality behind each fantasy. The fallacy of life was just meant to be. Look at where your mind is going, living all these years and still not knowing, waiting for life to be showing you the path, I laugh. So how can you curse God, you can't dodge his wrath, you're looking at magazines and wish that you'll have you're thinking life styles I'm starting to get mad, you see my smile but can't see the pain I've had, you'll dealing with the good while I've had to wallow in the bad.

How real is this, life is nothing but a dream, it don't mean a thing, it's nothing but a scheme.

Life is as life was meant to be.  Played out each day individually, played out by some mentally, when death is the only thing that'll set them free. You're seeing my dreams but I've had to endure things just to get here so don't judge a person based solely on what you fear, life is outside in instead of the other way around, it's never clear it's your fears that hold you down, it's like the circus which are you ringmaster or clown.  I've found I wasn't happy unless I was facing some kind of down, some kind of simple when I made the weak profound. Kept the mass's laughing cause I was the weak one, I was the meek one a strong brother turned into the geek-e one I'm not just talking about me cause I'm not the only one. The things we do to survive in this world, growing up to soon, waiting for that 1999 doom. We want to believe in things needing change; we want a life that's free of pain. Fame will never guaranty a life free of pain; I really don't think I could do this again, eternal sleep or another lifetime of shame; I'm of a tropical people so I can never be tamed, so can you hear me, can you feel this can you feel what has brought me to this. This is not let's make a deal but I will allow you one wish, love making with a kiss, or pick one from some other list. Either way you slice it, life is nice just like sex but at what price.

How real is this, life is nothing but a dream, it don't mean a thing, it's nothing but a scheme.

# Trees and Leaves

Trees and leaves clouding my mind just passing time just and escape a place to find
Trees and leaves like make believe and time just and escape a place to find
Tress and leaves

Trees and leaves you best believe don't be naive; I'm just like you everybody has a story to tell if you lived mine you'll call it hell, it's just as well I'm just a shell of the man that I once knew, it's true I was a young one carrying big guns blowing trees and sexing thieves for fun. A life on the run there's more to this you know I'm not done.

Trees and leaves clouding my mind just passing time just and escape a place to find
Trees and leaves like make believe and time just and escape a place to find
Tress and leaves

A cool breeze more trees more leaves much more make believe forgive me for I refuse to grieve. I choose to succeed. I need a new direction no more false affection but our lives are true lies until we die, so don't cry I lived this life one love two ex-wives, from sudden burst of rage born to hate born a renegade. I thought I'd never change but change is part of the game I came prepared so pass the flame.

Trees and leaves clouding my mind just passing time just and escape a place to find
Trees and leaves like make believe and time just and escape a place to find
Tress and leaves

Trees and leaves natures fruit for eve, why can't we have peace no D's, no G's just cheese, but here comes greed now it's fuck peace

74

I'm in this for me. Now everybody's at war no one can score, no one's making dollars any more we're all laying low or hiding no more high capping that's just the way shit happens this ain't even news, just another day in the life we choose. A few trips by the blues, cameo shots on the news I'll make you famous but then we both lose, I'd rather roll the gold an share some views.

Trees and leaves clouding my mind just passing time just and escape a place to find
Trees and leaves like make believe and time just and escape a place to find
Tress and leaves

# For My Pops

This is just something that I've always wanted to say to my pops, never even laid eyes on him, Hell I don't even know his name. I think I do but I'll never speak it tastes like shit and brings forth pain, so feel this with me.

I was born from a fucking that's why my life has been so disrupting dropped in 57 born needing and wanting if pain came with a charge I was born owing. Mama it's not really your fought born female you were just caught, I just blame my FAM for not facing up to the story. Got me guessing through this shit, piecing shit together another bastard child not knowing. So why ask me where my heads at which way in life am I going. Showing me that flow, am I suppose to believe now that my flow is flowing.

By the time I showed I was interested I was 17 and twisted, I wasn't looking for fatherly love I just wanted to know who he was, but you thought I was just a young fool wanting to play catch with pops after school. I just wanted to get rescued from myself before the streets swallowed me like everybody else I knew. No role figures just tricks and freaks and fake ass nigga's, wife beaters, weak ass's with heaters, just back shooters and closest racists, dope users more crooks in police cruisers, not in the back seat, driving and packing heat. Hey Pops, that was my life on six-trey street.

But hey Pops what do you care, you were off with your wife and real kids somewhere. So my pain never ended until I was befriended; by the dealers and killers in the hood, happy was pretending my tension increased not ending everything I saw seemed to be no fucking good. One of life's moments was on the way I was stabbed and shot at in the same fucking day. I felt like Dennis treated like a menace not to society just to myself I had to make a move fuck waiting on you and everybody else. My mother was off working all the time the answer was within me but I was blitzed or just out of my mind. I was just using or selling doing or bailing my mental me was failing, authority figures yelling, there was Veronique tranquility was compelling. Since it was the right thing to do Pops I followed you and was rebelling. Hey Pops you had what I didn't a choice, you didn't chose me but you didn't have to run. I didn't choose you either but I'm still your son. Hey Pops I know you had a reason within your own mind why you let a woman keep you away from your own bloodline, that's fine. I understand you have passed away so I'll show you more respect than you ever showed me and wont bash your weak ass today. R.I.P. dude, hey Pops that's all I have to say.

# Not That Day

I see your smile, I like your style but I feel a mile away, within my mind you're apart of every love game I play. I often think that today will be the day, but that's not your way. You have a star in your eyes that views you as his prize and you like it that way. Bonds that have grown to stay even though my feeling are persistent, they're tempting, this feeling is resistant to that little voice I won't listen. Your very presence is thrilling, your very essence is chilling, against all odds I'm willing. One mans lost is another mans killing, if he caught one of my ladies tripping he'd be tipping but that don't make it right not really.

That would be cheap I never want to regret, I don't see you as a cheap thrill of meaningless sex, so my mental me just reflex, I can't step to you not yet, I view you as the pinnacle as good as life can get. I can see you every time I close my eyes, even when I'm with my woman I can visualize me in your zone. You and I at home; even in a crowded room it's just you and I alone. My mental me plays this scene each and everyday in every imaginable way strange as it seems when I do see you my words are lost, I don't know what to say, so out of fear of looking like a fool I turn and go the other way. The last thing I want to do is for you to think all I want to do is to play. When all I really want to do is to love you each and everyday, is that okay; for now that love will have to wait for today is not that day.

# It's About Life

It ain't about the tears cause I can't cry no more
It ain't about the fears cause I wont lie no more
It ain't about the years cause I'll die for sure
So what's it about it's about life and in life I don't know

Heartaches, no breaks living a life that sometimes gives but more times takes, introducing my new love but she turned out to be fake; for that happiness that I seek I guess I'll have to wait. Lucifer called me but I can't make that date sell my soul for a goal but that's a foolish fate. That shit too will have to wait, I'm alone but not fending for a date. Pops wants to give me advice but this is life how can you enjoy the good times if you've never known strife.

It ain't about the tears cause I can't cry no more
It ain't about the fears cause I wont lie no more
It ain't about the years cause I'll die for sure
So what's it about it's about life and in life I don't know

Hustler games learned those things; six-trey was more about making dollars out of change. Partners dying while passing the flame reaching for heaters all because of a dame, now that's lame; When your whole world is the spot and you're living for the block now that's a true shame, dying for the game, dying for pride, killing to hide our own mental lapse's, the street life ain't no game it's filled with traps and devices. We've learned to live with the roaches and the mice's and all kinds of sick ass vices. That's just life so tell me what life is.

It ain't about the tears cause I can't cry no more
It ain't about the fears cause I wont lie no more
It ain't about the years cause I'll die for sure
So what's it about it's about life and in life I don't know

Corroded my heart has imploded my mental me feels explosive
that's just how clicks be when life has you supposing, just hoping.
But mine was a quick hit, a nickel bag fix I was drugging, I watch
my dreams die but I was to high to cry. I rebounded to say
goodbye to that flame, instead of user I turn producer in the game
that's the same madness with just a different name, This is life
ain't no substitute for the pain, no hiding or running law abiding
or gunning, to survive you realize your inner strength stunning,
but life is the prize you get just one only, homie.

It ain't about the tears cause I can't cry no more
It ain't about the fears cause I wont lie no more
It ain't about the years cause I'll die for sure
So what's it about it's about life and in life I don't know
Dark Side

Raised by the church and females; somehow I got twisted between
doing what's right and living life right, I didn't listen. I remember
dialing numbers that were always unlisted. Being pulled to the left
because right just resisted, I never fretted never knew fear I don't
regret it I just wish I could speak and someone would hear, not
just sounds but my pain clear. Not until it's all fucked up or I'm
used up dose someone pull me near. Then hold their hand out and
say pay me I brought you here.

But that's alright that's life, there are two sides when you realize
all life is not in the dark side, but the bright side is confused with
the right side and false pride. I feel stronger and maybe I'll live
longer in the dark side

To much watching and seeing hating and needing, still seeing
when seeing is not the same as believing and believing leaves your
heart peeving. Or, is that seething. One step before grieving that
brings me back to seeing and believing. We're wrapped up in that
faith shit and wont lend a hand without some form of repayment.
Praying daily to maintain your mental grip. I feel like I'm one
step from making tricks abandon ship, but that ain't my

statement. Waiting for reparations but why get aide or that cheese and powdered egg supplement. Dying for nothing but a cause is all I can get, so I say fuck you and put my foot the only place that it'll fit. In front of me on the ground, I've dances so much no more go a rounds my mental me is like my bank account is sound.

But that's alright that's life, there are two sides when you realize all life is not in the dark side, but the bright side is confused with the right side and false pride. I feel stronger and maybe I'll live longer in the dark side

My dreams just seem to miss me resist me, just knowing me the world seemed fitted against me. Believing in shits that just seem to click in clicks but acted beneath me. I keep needing people that never needed me I'm right in front of you but you're not seeing me, even when I speak clearly you're not believing me. I love some of this dearly but sometimes in life I feel life is fearing me or is that because the end is nearing me. It's just I'm not understanding the demanding effect that life has placed on me, then giving the loss's vs. the wins I reflex with negativity. But sometimes life shows life's positive shit to me then 10 year olds lose control and the classroom is shot up. Then we blame it on the way he or she was brought. Life is survival of the fittest and I never want to be caught up.

But that's alright that's life, there are two sides when you realize all life is not in the dark side, but the bright side is confused with the right side and false pride. I feel stronger and maybe I'll live longer in the dark side

# Nothing But Love (NBL)

How real is this, when it's nothing but love for love is nothing but
a curse,
Show me a man that's known love I'll show you a man that's
known hurt.
How real is this, when it's nothing but love for love is a part time
job with full time work, it's sometimes fun but more times work,
nothing but love is nothing but work, nothing like love for love is
nothing but a curse.

My mental me plays a vision of reality, my fantasy was love when
love was never to be. I lied, I tried to pretend heaven was within
my reach, but then again everything that starts must end. The
pains in my heart but what part of love makes me think that you
were even my friend. When forever I seek I met your body but
when will we really meet. I've lost some battles in life but love
made me feel defeat, the next moment weak, with you I was
struggling without you I feel complete.

How real is this, when it's nothing but love for love is nothing but
a curse,
Show me a man that's known love I'll show you a man that's
known hurt.
How real is this, when it's nothing but love for love is a part time
job with full time work, it's sometimes fun but more times work,
nothing but love is nothing but work, nothing like love for love is
nothing but a curse.

It's not all-bad pain and thangs there's sometimes sex to ease the
strain. The challenges of blending two hearts comes back again;
with no one communicating or just one of you faking that thin
line that defines love just loves to have you hating, needlessly
waiting. Even with a choice of colors it's red we're showing one
another, but it's sometimes green. Instead of love it's envy you're
holding yesterday against me, using sex as a weapon orally for my
birthday but other days I'm just guessing. This is what I wanted

so this must be my lesson, one moment you're touching me the next you're stressing me. Now you're telling friends that you've never known a brother such as me. That's just more proof for the truth that even on sunny days sometimes we can't see.

How real is this, when it's nothing but love for love is nothing but a curse,
Show me a man that's known love I'll show you a man that's known hurt.
How real is this, when it's nothing but love for love is a part time job with full time work, it's sometimes fun but more times work, nothing but love is nothing but work, nothing like love for love is nothing but a curse.

# When Life Was My Friend

Oh I think about my life and where I've been, a time in life when life was my friend.
How can I go there again, I wanna go back to then
That time of life when life was my friend

I'm mentally cruising another night of endo and zooming, another day of doing nothing special just watching my life's clock moving, nine-to-fiving and losing. I seldom smile street life consumed my childhood so now, I'm in survival mode I don't feel proud. I'm kissing ass's on the mass's just to be allowed to pay my car note and rent, watching cable and wonder where opportunity went, I was never living life I was just hell bent I picked up my bible and this is the message that I was sent.

Oh I think about my life and where I've been, a time in life when life was my friend.
How can I go there again, I wanna go back to then
That time of life when life was my friend

From nightlife to constantly stone never home fast lane downing black label to ease my pain, to no doubts never sleeping just night passing out. Now that bills due now I'm waking up instead of just coming to. Thought life was shaping up but reality blew through, left me nine-to-fiving in place of life I'm surviving. Where once I was striding, never knowing pain, now experiencing hurt I'm told to be thankful but a job ain't nothing but work. Shit just don't happen just because you search, I'm missing my childhood must be something to it everywhere I'm looking I'm seeing a church.

Oh I think about my life and where I've been, a time in life when life was my friend.
How can I go there again, I wanna go back to then
That time of life when life was my friend

Life is truly astounding many wrong turns have left me sounding bitter when the sweetness of hope has me surrounded. That street life and flame left my heart pounding now a new generation of fools are clowning more booze, more drugs, more gangs, more people choose thangs to drown their sorrow, stop their tomorrows. Again now my bill is due for living on time borrowed, damn I could have been you, what if you wanted the same things too, burning trees and leaves, sexing thieves a teen smart juvie with teen years experience makes me naïve. Pick your idols wisely what a fool believes. Still I refuse to grieve for as long as I'm breathing I'll have what I need.

Oh I think about my life and where I've been, a time in life when life was my friend.
How can I go there again, I wanna go back to then
That time of life when life was my friend

# What's Wrong With this Poem?

It's like a part of me has died even though I suffer not so many wish for the little shit I got, still I lie awake depressed at night during the day I smile to conceal my fright. What is this with me why dose the world feel against me, I put down the flame and alcohol to clear my head, but it seems it got more cloudy or is it just crowded instead. Either way my sober mind feels misled makes me think back to what I've heard before being re-played I'm in the sun I'm burning up my world is turning up I pause this is what I wanted Hell is hot now I'm searching for some shade. I said no when the devil asked me to sell my soul, this time I asked he said no I took to long, this is my life now tell me what went wrong, damn what's wrong with this song what's wrong with this poem?

Ain't no sunshine replays again and again mama forgive father can't I was just a kid, that was just one sin I've felt a few victories, more loss's bleeding for some fucked up causes just cost me, the purpose being lost to me. No one to talk to even my brother walked from me alone and on my on, brought by one so one is all I've known. Watching movies then reading about history, I realized this world was built on someone's misery. It took sometime to realize that it was me lying to me, trying to be everything in life that I shouldn't be. So when you look at me what do you see, don't answer that for some things are better just thought to be. The color purple, purple haze or purple rain, without purple life would be strange without colors maybe we all could gain. I said no when the devil asked me to sell my soul he said no when I asked stand in line but the line was to lone, this is my life now tell me what went wrong. Damn, tell me what's wrong with this song, what's wrong with this poem?

It don't matter what you've done it's about what you do, but don't look surprise when you realize that what you do only matters to you. Getting caught up in life from hazy to crazy, I learned to sidestep tricks cause tricks don't faze me. I never asked for help I struggled but depended on self to me beggars are lazy and that wasn't me. Mad-Dog would listen tried to help but had a lot on his plate I was just his little cousin grown up now to face a jacked up fate, my brothers in the background dissing out hate, I know you mean well for me but that shit is just to late. My prior wasn't Richard it was assault, two dudes that were bitches I didn't run and got caught. I'm not guilty but it was my fault. So now I sit in Michigan writing about my shit and where I've been, trying hard not to live that shit again, you can't run from life just your fake ass friends. I said no the first time the devil asked me to sell my soul, he said wait on God and I'll leave you alone, I'm still waiting I just need faith to be strong this is my life now tell me what went wrong. Damn, what's wrong with this song, what's wrong with this poem?

# Back Into It

I'm trying my best to keep from getting back into it, this nine-to-five shit makes me wanna do it, My life I don't want to ruin it, sometimes it seems I don't know what I'm doing, working everyday I still feel like I'm losing.
But I keep on doing it, just to keep from getting back into it.

Hey Thelma I know I sometimes I sound bitter, it's just that I'm the youngest of your litter. Street life and street fights making a killing cause the money is right. I've been there before but I'm no killer, hell I'm no dealer, I have no excuse cause making that paper, sexing women, just that life style makes me willing. When I look at the choice's I'm giving what choice? You either flush or you ain't. You're making a deposit or you're robbing the bank. Those that can, do the rest of us want to but can't she's either a dyme piece or a stank.

I'm trying my best to keep from getting back into it, this nine-to-five shit makes me wanna do it, My life I don't want to ruin it, sometimes it seems I don't know what I'm doing, working everyday I still feel like I'm losing.
But I keep on doing it, just to keep from getting back into it.

Climbing life always takes more time, falling seems to go faster, finding success is a steady climb unless you're tricking or confessing, second guessing or just unsure of yourself. A fake ass wanna be flexing. Do you fit in then get in or get in then fit in, I'm just checking where I'm from knowing the difference is your first lesson or is that your first blessing. Either way these are not just street rhythms about street crimes or street times these lines are about my life and times just about making paper, that nine-to-five is a work now get paid latter capper. Here I go again the sum of two equals which one is greater.

I'm trying my best to keep from getting back into it, this nine-to-five shit makes me wanna do it, My life I don't want to ruin it, sometimes it seems I don't know what I'm doing, working everyday I still feel like I'm losing.
But I keep on doing it, just to keep from getting back into it.

It's always poor folks with poor voice seeing riches but receiving no choice. Until you turn around in full force, a .44, or cardboard box leaving your FAM with remorse. Keep believing that shit the media tells you; you better check your source. I was living life like this was my last night, no matter what shit just didn't seem right, Now I'm nine-to-fiving got credit cards no cash, that's just strength with no might now I don't even have a stash. I feel like I'm fronting not having but always wanting, trapped in a work life rush, never flushed. Just flushed down that toilet of life, existing in a world that'll never treat a brother right. For now I'm avoiding that county jail dodging a rival crews bounty on a trip to hell so for one more day I'll live trapped in this shell.

I'm trying my best to keep from getting back into it, this nine-to-five shit makes me wanna do it, My life I don't want to ruin it, sometimes it seems I don't know what I'm doing, working everyday I still feel like I'm losing.
But I keep on doing it, just to keep from getting back into it.

# Love Is Gone

She was sipping Kaluha and cream, a living dream rolling endo I liked her flow from the go, I just didn't know what I was in for. She had charm so I didn't raise my guard I macking hard, no cause for alarm. Picture perfect yo, I said fuck it what's the harm here I go.  From moment one we clicked, I said this is it that conversating led to dating, days of styling the latest fashions, to nights of passion. Minds racing but I'm into this into action, chilling into TV no sound music for the background I'm just reading the captions. I'm in a zone I didn't what happen. Days are now apart now shit just seems bent; nights are back to back or arguments.  How could what was so right now be so wrong it's like that after the love is gone, the love is gone.

Now shit is just whacked, ain't no moving ahead or backing up, I know when enough is enough. I hate to abandon ship but I've had I've had enough. All this arguing will lead to fighting, you just don't know how close I came to hitting you and that's frightening. To know hate and love are interchangeable, from one moment to the next this shit is unexplainable.  When I tried to stay there's no peace at home, when I tried to leave you wouldn't leave me alone. Smashing my windows, cutting up my clothes, dissing my jones, calling and hanging up the phone. Trying to get me touched by the police, that shit is just wrong, damn you went from turning my mind to turning against me, you went as far as fucking my enemy. How could so much weakness come from a woman so strong, it's like that after the love is gone, the love is gone.

It's not all you I did my part, I open the door and you cracked my heart, if you could you'd cracked my head but instead you talked to the media and said some shit that was just between us. So much for love, so much for trust. It's either your way or bust confessing in a moment of lust the jacked up part is now I see, You didn't play me I played myself waking up to find out I got very little creditability left. No rules when it comes to love and war, that's what I get for loving a stranger, my shit wont be like before. My

90

grief couldn't be any planer, I lived a street life but fell to bedroom danger. We've been apart for a while but I still feel anger. It's still in my smile and now reflected in my lifestyle love can make you feel weak where you were once strong. Everybody plays the fool; if you try to love after the love is gone, the love is gone.

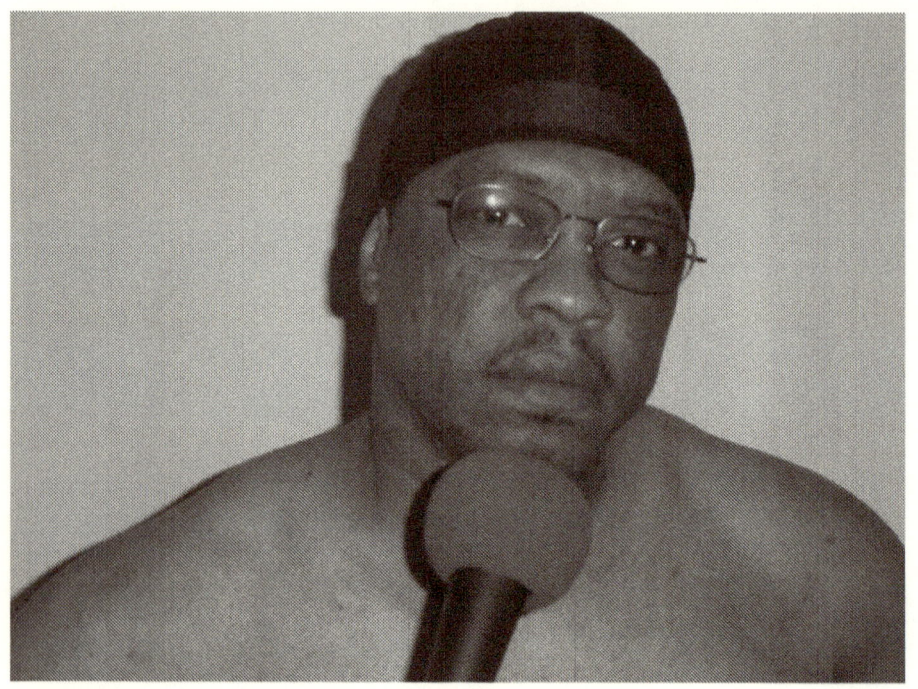

*LAYTON*

*LAYTON*

# About the Author

Raised in the streets of Chicago's Southside Layton has turned a lifetime of experiences into his first book of poetic magic. Feel blessed in that you get to just read this while Layton had to endure, survive, and experience this. Now from the streets to the paper lines feel what has made Layton the man that he is today. One Life So Many Dreams don't just read this feel the experience as reality reaches out to grab you through poetic rhythms about street life and street times.

One Life So Many Dreams the magic is just beginning,

## One Life So Many Dreams.